Focus on Australia

Natalie Hyde

A Crabtree Forest Book

Author: Natalie Hyde

Series research and development:
Janine Deschenes

Editorial director: Kathy Middleton

Editor: Crystal Sikkens

Proofreader: Melissa Boyce

Design: Tammy McGarr

Print and production coordinator:
Katherine Berti

IMAGE CREDITS

Shutterstock:
ChameleonsEye, pgs 3, 4, 34, 36 (bottom), 45 (bottom); Serge Goujon, p 15 (top); myphotobank.com.au, p 15 (bottom); Ingus Kruklitis, p 20 (top); fritz16, pgs 21 (all images), 37 (bottom); Mystic Stock Photography, p 23 (top); BigDane, p 24 (middle); LittlePanda29, p 24 (bottom); Benny Marty, pgs 25 (top right), 36 (top), 45 (top); Maurizio De Mattei, p 25 (bottom right; Aldo Manganarop 25 (bottom); Philip Schubert, p 26 (bottom); Jackson Stock Photography, p 29; Jimbo_Cymru, p 35 (middle); katacarix, p 35 (bottom); Tooykrub, p 37 (top); Di Vincenzo, p 38 (bottom); valerialina, p 39; J Mundy, p 40; Wirestock Creators, p 43 (bottom); Farizun Amrod Saad, p 44;

Wikimedia Commons: Public Domain, p 18 (top); Robert Hawker Dowling, p 18 (bottom); Algernon Talmage, p 19 (top), Creative Commons, p 18 (middle), p 22 (bottom), p 27 (top)

Crabtree Publishing

crabtreebooks.com 800-387-7650

In Canada: We acknowledge the financial support of the Government of Canada through the Canada Book Fund for our publishing activities.

Hardcover	978-1-0398-0645-0
Paperback	978-1-0398-0671-9
Ebook (pdf)	978-1-0398-0697-9
Epub	978-1-0398-0724-2

Published in Canada
Crabtree Publishing
616 Welland Avenue
St. Catharines, Ontario
L2M 5V6

Published in the United States
Crabtree Publishing
347 Fifth Avenue
Suite 1402-145
New York, New York, 10016

Library and Archives Canada Cataloguing in Publication
Available at Library and Archives Canada

Library of Congress Cataloging-in-Publication Data
Available at the Library of Congress

Printed in the U.S.A./012023/CG20220815

Contents

Introduction

Sheepshearing

It is a busy September morning on a sheep station in southwestern Australia. Springtime in the **southern hemisphere** is the busiest time for shearing. The shearing team of eight arrives at 7 a.m. and consists of four shearers and four roustabouts. Roustabouts gather, pick, and press the wool after it has been sheared from the sheep. The shearers use electric shears to remove the wool in one piece from the sheep on the shearing stands. Wool from the belly of the sheep goes into a separate bucket because it is finer. Roustabouts take the **fleece** and pick out the dirt and poop. Professional shearers can each do about 150 sheep in an eight-hour day.

Shearers travel from station to station across the southeast and southwest of Australia where most of the sheep stations are located. Spring is their busiest time, but there are shearing jobs year-round because some breeds are shorn twice a year, and young sheep are sometimes shorn in the summer to make them more comfortable. The sheep industry in Australia, both meat and wool, is worth more than $8 billion AUD ($5.5 billion USD).

When done correctly, getting sheared is not much different than getting a haircut.

Kings Canyon is a popular hiking spot located in the Northern Territory on Australia's mainland.

A Snapshot of Australia

Australia is the only country in the world that is also a continent. It is the sixth-largest country and smallest continent. It is also the largest island on Earth. It is made up of mainland Australia, the island of Tasmania, and several other smaller islands. The capital city is Canberra, which is located in the southeast. Australia is surrounded by three oceans: the Indian Ocean to the west, the Pacific Ocean to the north and east, and the Southern Ocean to the south. About 26 million people call Australia their home. Australia's soil often looks red. This is because the hot, dry climate is the perfect condition for iron ore in the soil and rocks to rust. This gives the ground its reddish color.

A field of lavender grows in the red soil in Tasmania.

States and Territories

Australia is divided into six states and two territories. States have their own state governments, but the territories are managed by the federal government.

Western Australia (WA) is the largest state, taking up about one-third of mainland Australia. Its capital, Perth, sits right on the western coast. The region has valuable diamond and gold mines. To the northeast of WA is the Northern Territory. In the north of this territory the climate is **tropical**, but to the south it is **semi-arid desert**.

In the northeast, bordering the Northern Territory, is Queensland. It has the wettest and most tropical climate. Brisbane is the capital. It is the second-largest state—it is almost twice the size of Texas. Called the Sunshine State, it is a popular destination for tourists, especially to visit the Great Barrier Reef off the east coast.

In the South

New South Wales (NSW) is a state in the southeast of mainland Australia. Its capital city is Sydney. It has mountains along the coast and plains in the interior. The far south coast of the state is called the Sapphire Coast, named for the beautiful color of the sea and sky.

In the southeast corner of the country is the mountainous state of Victoria with its capital city Melbourne. Victoria is separated from NSW to the north by the Murray River. To the west, it shares a border with South Australia. South Australia is one of the driest states, but along the southern coast is a narrow strip of land that has more water and is fertile. This is where the capital Adelaide sits.

Tasmania is an island state that lies 150 miles (240 km) south of the state of Victoria, across the Bass Strait. Hobart is the capital and the island has beautiful mountains, lakes, and coastlines. Most of the land is protected in national parks and reserves.

Australia's capital, Canberra, lies along the Molonglo River in the Australian Capital Territory (ACT). The Australian Capital Territory is surrounded by the state of New South Wales. This small territory is about 910 square miles (2,360 sq. km).

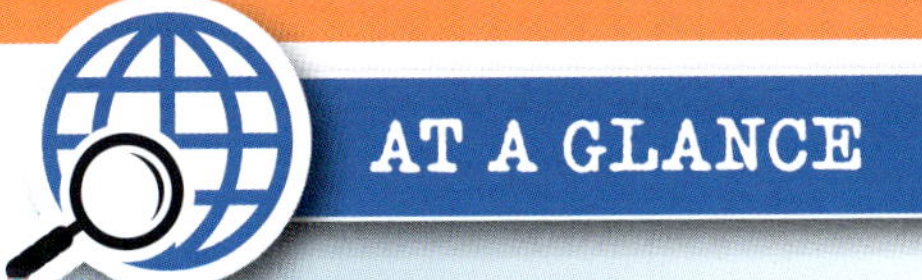

- **OFFICIAL NAME:** Commonwealth of Australia
- **NATIONAL CAPITAL:** Canberra
- **POPULATION:** 25,892,000
- **OFFICIAL LANGUAGES:** English
- **LAND AREA:** 2,969,906 square miles (7,692,021 sq. km)

CHAPTER 1 The Land

From the air, Australia may look like one huge desert, but that is not the case. While it is the flattest and driest continent, other than Antarctica, Australia also contains many mountains, rain forests, and a lot of fertile land.

Many Mountains

There are several mountain ranges throughout the mainland of Australia. The largest is the Great Dividing Range. It is called this because it separates the **drainage basins** of rivers. This mountain range runs the length of the eastern coastline, from Queensland all the way to Victoria. The Australian Alps are part of the Great Dividing Range. The Alps are in the southern portion and include Australia's highest peaks.

The Outback

Two-thirds of the western part of the country consists of the Western Plateau. This ancient **rock shield** is flat, sandy, or stony ground where rain rarely falls. There are shrubs and a few grasses. Even though it is a harsh landscape, parts of the plateau support one of the world's greatest wool industries.

Between the Western Plateau and the Eastern Mountain ranges are the Central Lowlands. These are flat, low-lying plains. Rivers flow through this region after heavy rains, but the rest of the year the riverbeds are dry. In the southern part of the lowlands grass grows high enough for sheep and cattle. In the northern lowlands it is much drier. The dry Western Plateau and lowlands are what Australians call the Outback.

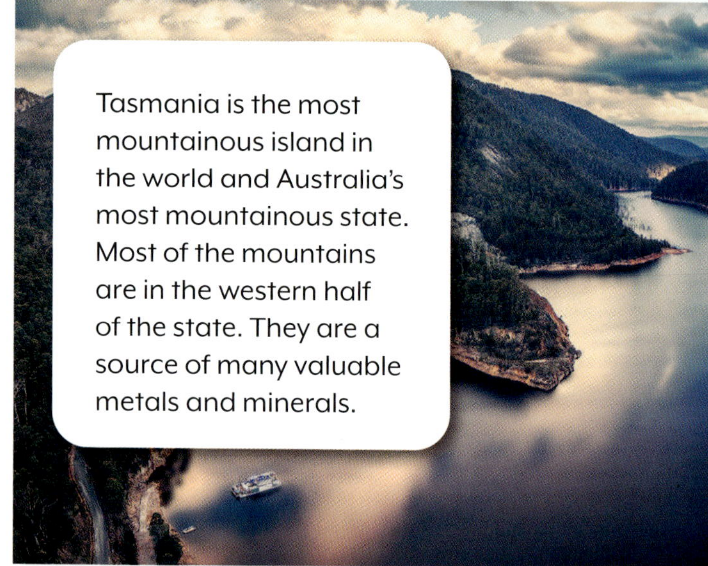

Tasmania is the most mountainous island in the world and Australia's most mountainous state. Most of the mountains are in the western half of the state. They are a source of many valuable metals and minerals.

Different rock formations can be seen in the Outback.

The Nullarbor Plain in South Australia is the world's largest limestone plain. It contains more than 250 limestone caves.

Closer Look

Fraser Island

Fraser Island in Queensland is the world's largest sand island. It has an area of 454,674 acres (184,000 hectares) that stretches more than 76 miles (123 km) long. Because of its rare and unique features, it was listed as a **UNESCO World Heritage site** in 1992. It is the only place in the world where tall rain forests grow on sand dunes at elevations of over 656 feet (200 m). The island has 72 different-colored sands but most are reds and yellows. Scattered across the island are more than 100 freshwater lakes surrounded by white sand beaches. In 2021, its name officially changed to K'gari, meaning "paradise" in the Butchulla language. The Butchulla people were the island's first inhabitants.

On the Edge

As an island, Australia is a country with no land borders. It has a coastline 22,258 miles (35,821 km) long. That means the coast plays a major role in the settlement, industry, tourism, and climate of the country.

The Great Barrier Reef

Off the northeastern coast of Australia is the world's largest coral reef: the Great Barrier Reef. It is made up of more than 3,000 individual reef systems. There are also hundreds of tropical islands and coral **cays** in the system. It is one of the world's most popular tourist destinations. Visitors can scuba dive, snorkel, enjoy glass-bottomed boat rides, helicopter tours, whale watching, swimming with dolphins, or just enjoy the beautiful beaches.

The Great Ocean Road stretches 150 miles (240 km) along the southeastern coast of Australia. It goes past soaring limestone pillars called the 12 Apostles that are 10 to 20 million years old.

Fishing

The waters around Australia provide both commercial and recreational fishing. The fishing industry, including mollusks and crustaceans, produces around 330,000 tons (300,000 metric tons) of seafood each year. Recreational fishing is one of the most popular outdoor activities in the country. Fishers often spend about $10 billion AUD ($7 billion USD) a year on the sport.

Warm Water and Air

Ocean currents flowing along the coast bring warmer water southward around the island. This impacts the temperature, rainfall, and fish migration. The warmer temperatures can cause droughts or floods. Sometimes **monsoon** winds in the Indian Ocean push warmer air to Australia. This can reduce rainfall, which may lead to large and devastating bushfires. Bushfires happen regularly in Australia. Some plants have adapted to rely on bushfires to reproduce, such as the Banksia tree. Fire causes its cones to open and release seeds. However, fires still destroy thousands of acres of forests and kill animals every year.

These cones on a Banksia tree have opened and released seeds after a fire in Victoria.

A coral reef might look like plants or rocks, but they are actually animals.

About 17 percent of Australia is forest. About three-quarters of the forests are eucalypt trees.

Natural Resources

Natural resources are an important part of Australia's economy. Metals and minerals in the ground are the most valuable natural resources in Australia. There are about 19 different minerals, including iron ore, nickel, gold, uranium, diamonds, and zinc, mined in almost 400 mines across the country. Coal is Australia's largest energy resource. Around 60 percent of electricity across the country is produced in coal-fired power stations. Queensland has the most coal production, followed by NSW, South Australia, Tasmania, and Western Australia. Most of Australia's mining products are **exported** to China, South Korea, Japan, and India.

Opals

Australia is the largest producer of opals—95 percent of the world's supply comes from Australia. This gemstone is formed deep down in the ground where **silica**-rich water seeps into cracks in the rocks and hardens over millions of years. The opal fields lie in Queensland, NSW, and South Australia. The most valuable are black opals found only in NSW. These gemstones show a rainbow of colors against a dark background. Opals are used in jewelry, and they bring in more than $200 million AUD ($138 million USD) to the Australian economy each year.

Eureka!

In 1885, gold was discovered near Kimberley, Western Australia, which started a gold rush. A second gold rush occurred after a major discovery in 1892 in Coolgardie, WA. The Boddington Gold Mine in WA is Australia's largest gold mine, producing more than 24 tons (22 metric tons) of gold per year.

Natural Gas

Natural gas is a fossil fuel formed deep in the ground. It is colorless, odorless, and highly **flammable**. In Australia, most gas basins are off the north shore of Western Australia, throughout central Australia, and off the south shores of Victoria and South Australia. Australia has 44 times more natural gas than it uses. It ships almost all of its excess natural gas to Asia, including China, Japan, and South Korea.

The Torrens Island Power Station near Adelaide in South Australia burns natural gas in eight steam turbines.

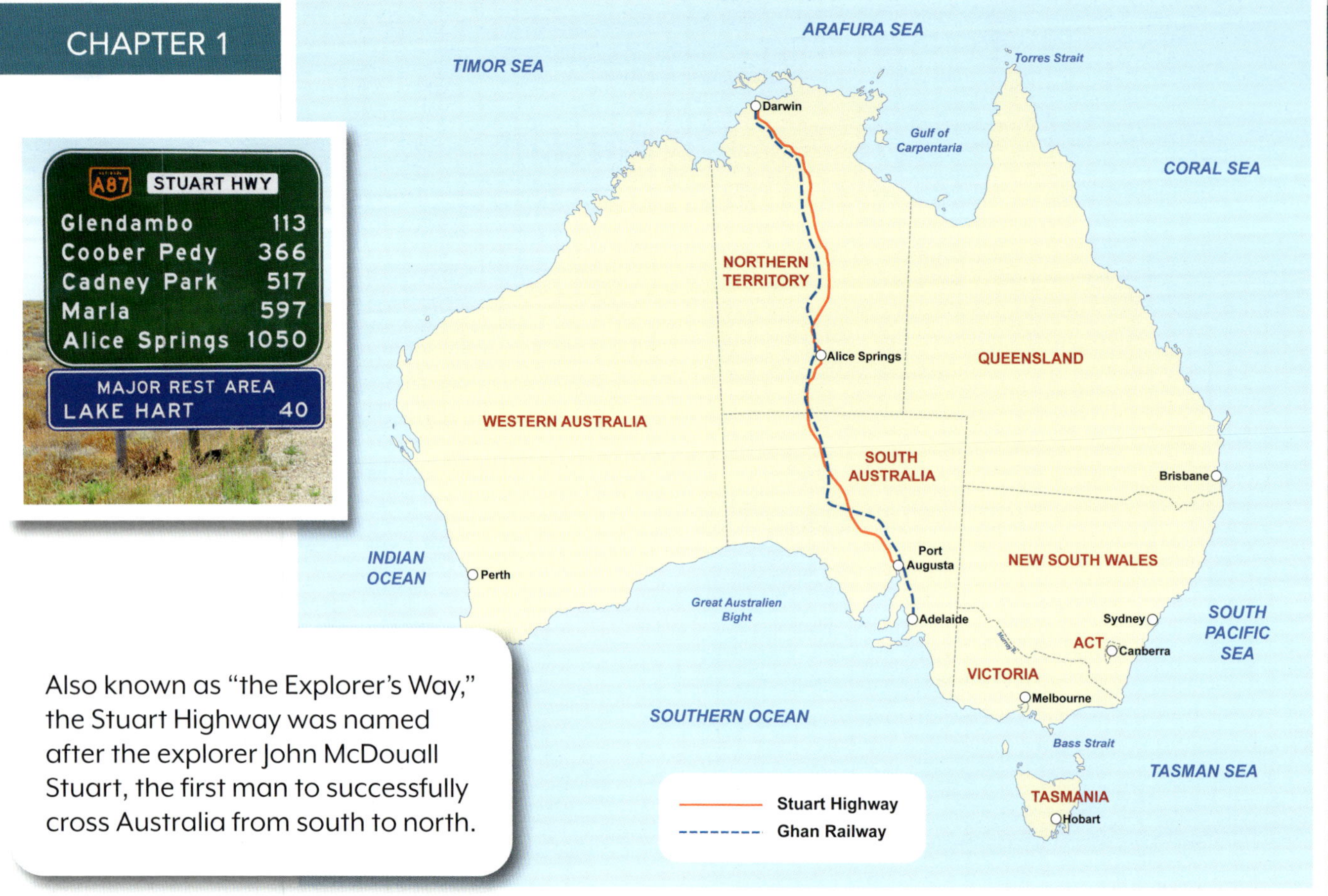

Also known as "the Explorer's Way," the Stuart Highway was named after the explorer John McDouall Stuart, the first man to successfully cross Australia from south to north.

Settlements

Australia is one of the least **densely** populated countries in the world. There are only seven people per square mile (three per sq. km). This is because the interior of the country is mainly desert, which creates very difficult living conditions. The harsh climate and lack of water mean many of the settlements in the Outback center around mining industries. Less than 5 percent of Australia's population lives in the Outback.

Because the interior of the country is so hot and dry, 80 percent of people in Australia live along the coast. People first settled near the coast because it provided access to transportation, food, water, and business opportunities. The ocean also meant cooler temperatures and more rainfall for crops.

Getting Around

The first railway in Australia was built in 1854 in Melbourne. Shortly after that, railways began to spring up all around the country. There were problems, however, because different areas had different track gauges. A track gauge is the distance between the two rails of a track. When these lines were connected, the tracks and trains were not **compatible**.

Once cities were founded, rough paths were improved to make a road system and bridges. There is now a national highway system that connects all major cities and regional centers in all states and territories. One portion of this system is the Stuart Highway. It spans the country right through the middle, from Port Augusta in the south to Darwin in the north.

The Stuart Highway is one of Australia's longest roads. It passes through some of the same cities as The Ghan train route.

Closer Look

The Ghan

The Ghan is a train that runs between the northern and southern coasts. Built in 1929, it originally took passengers and supplies from Adelaide to Alice Springs. In 1980, the rail line was finally extended north to Darwin. Today, it is mostly a passenger train for tourism. The trip takes approximately 53 hours and 15 minutes.

Climate Zones

Because of its large size, Australia has many different climate zones. It lies in the southern hemisphere, which means December and January are the hottest months. Winter's coldest months are July and August.

Along the northern coast, the climate is tropical. It is hot and humid in the summer and warm and dry in the winter. The temperature rarely goes below 64 °F (18 °C). It is covered in tropical rain forests and tropical grasslands. Along the southern coast is a **temperate** zone. This climate is cooler with mild summers and sometimes rainy winters. **Vegetation** in the temperate zone is mostly eucalypt forests.

The center of the country is the **arid** zone. There, temperatures can reach 122 °F (50 °C) and rain may not fall for years. There are still plants and animals that thrive there, including grasses, saltbushes, kangaroos, wild dogs called dingoes, and bats.

Although we think of Australia as hot—and it is—the Australian Alps, a mountain range in southeast Australia, can get up to 14 inches (36 cm) of snow each winter. People enjoy sports such as skiing and snowboarding.

Warm, Windy Weather

Warm ocean currents can create severe storms called cyclones. A cyclone is a system of winds rotating around a low-pressure center. The clouds and strong winds bring heavy rains that can cause wind damage and flooding.

Global warming is affecting the climate of Australia. It has warmed by more than 1.8 °F (1 °C) since 1910. While that doesn't sound like much, 1 degree can make storms much worse, prolong wildfire season, damage coral reefs, and cause sea levels to rise with melting ice sheets. In 2019, bushfires in Australia were the worst they have ever been. Called the Black Summer, bushfires that year destroyed 60–80 million acres (24–32 million hectares), more than 5,900 buildings, and killed at least 34 people.

CHAPTER 2

Development

Australia's First Peoples

Indigenous peoples have lived in Australia for at least 65,000 years. Two main groups make up the Indigenous population in Australia. Torres Strait Islander peoples inhabit the islands of the Torres Strait region, in the Pacific Ocean north of Queensland. Aboriginal peoples come from Australia's mainland, Tasmania, and other islands. There are many different Aboriginal and Torres Strait Islander groups, each with distinct languages and cultures.

The first Indigenous peoples to come to Australia either walked over land bridges formed by lower seas or arrived in boats. They were mainly hunter-gatherers. This means they **foraged** for their food and moved from place to place following animals to hunt. At the time of the arrival of Europeans, there were an estimated 320,000 Indigenous peoples. Most were living in the southeast and in the Murray River valley. In 1897, the government enacted a law that forced Indigenous peoples onto reservations. By restricting their movements, it disrupted their traditions of living and hunting.

The Gwion Gwion rock paintings located in Kimberley, Western Australia, are believed to be 12,000 years old.

Aboriginal people in Tasmania were cut off from mainland Australia for thousands of years due to a rise in the sea level of the Bass Strait.

Closer Look

Britain's Penal Colony

The arrival of the 11 ships on January 26, 1788, is celebrated as the founding of the country. This day is celebrated each year with music festivals and fireworks. Recently, there has been controversy around the day as it signifies the date that Indigenous peoples began to lose their land and rights.

In 1770, British explorer James Cook landed at Botany Bay and claimed it for Britain, naming the area New South Wales. Because Australia was so remote and British jails were full, it was seen as the perfect place to use as a **penal colony**. In 1788, 11 ships under Captain Arthur Phillip arrived at Port Jackson, also known as Sydney Harbour. The ships, known as the First Fleet, were carrying convicts—criminals convicted of small crimes. The majority of the convicts were poor and **illiterate** and victims of the harsh poor laws in Britain. Some were as young as nine years old. Cities were planned around their use as places for convicts, with forts to hold them, as well as agricultural and work camps. Sydney was the first penal colony. Penal outstations in Newcastle, Moreton Bay (which became Brisbane), and Port Arthur on the island of Tasmania were later established. Prisoners could earn their "ticket of leave" if they could support themselves with work or by growing food. This would allow them to start their lives over. Convicts were often used as free labor to build the new colony.

The last convict ship arrived in 1868 but free settlers were already arriving. The gold rush in 1851 brought hundreds of thousands of prospectors and miners to Australia.

The penal outstation in Port Arthur, Tasmania, was originally a flour mill and granary before being converted to a penitentiary in the 1850s.

The Sydney Opera House became a UNESCO World Heritage site in 2007.

Rival Cities

From its start as the first penal colony, Sydney grew to become the country's first city in 1842. The population increased even more after gold was discovered in 1851. Today, Sydney is the largest city in the country and one of the best known. Its most recognizable features include the Sydney Harbour Bridge and the Sydney Opera House, both located on Sydney Harbour. For more than 200 years, Sydney Harbour has been one of the most important trading ports in the South Pacific.

Melbourne was originally a meeting place of several Aboriginal groups of the Kulin people. John Batman, an Australian rancher, negotiated a **treaty** with elders of the area to buy land around Port Phillip. The settlement was named Melbourne in 1837 and remained small until gold was discovered nearby in the 1850s. The city swelled in size, making it the largest and wealthiest city at the time. Sydney's population eventually grew and surpassed Melbourne as the largest city. Sydney and Melbourne have had a long-standing rivalry as Australia's two largest cities. This competitive nature can often be seen in sports events.

Melbourne's central business district overlooks the Yarra River.

A Water Hole in the Desert

Alice Springs, originally called *Mparntwe* by the Aboriginal Arrernte people, is a remote town in Australia's Northern Territory. It began as the name of a water hole near a telegraph station halfway up the Overland Telegraph Line. The Overland Telegraph Line was constructed in 1871 and ran from Adelaide in the south to Darwin in the north. It followed the path taken by explorer John McDouall Stuart, the first person to cross the harsh center of the country. This line was soon linked to the Java-Darwin Telegraph Line, connecting Australia to Asia and Europe. Eventually the Alice Springs area grew into a bigger settlement after gold was found nearby in 1887. Today, Alice Springs is home to more than 30,000 people.

Coober Pedy produces about 70 percent of the world's opals.

Guests of Coober Pedy can stay in this underground hotel.

Closer Look

Underground City

Coober Pedy was founded in 1920, five years after opals were discovered in the area. Located in the Outback, temperatures in summer can climb to 118 °F (48 °C). There is very little rain, so sandstorms are a usual occurrence. For shelter and to avoid the heat, many of Coober Pedy's homes are built underground. Buildings, furniture, and sometimes even indoor swimming pools are carved out of the surrounding sandstone. About 60 percent of the 3,500 city residents spend their days underground, enjoying constant temperatures of about 74 °F (23 °C).

An underground home is carved out of the rock in Coober Pedy.

Mandarins are grown in all states in Australia.

Farming and Agriculture

The oldest industry in Australia is farming. Researchers have found some evidence that Indigenous peoples not only hunted and gathered their food, but also cultivated yams, sweet potatoes, millet, and "bush onions."

The convict ships from Britain not only brought prisoners, they also brought livestock. The first sheep farms were at Sydney Cove. Today, the Australian wool industry is worth almost $3.5 billion AUD ($2.4 billion USD). The major agricultural products are grains and oilseeds, meat, sugar, cotton, wool, and dairy.

Mining

The first mines were created in 1791, only three years after the First Fleet arrived with convicts. Coal was found near Newcastle in NSW. It was used for cooking and heat, and then steam power. The first exported coal was sent to India in 1799. Australia is now the largest exporter of coal in the world. Coal-fired power plants provide most of the electricity in Australia. The use of coal is **controversial**. The carbon dioxide **emitted** by coal plants contributes to climate change.

Lead and copper were the first metals to be mined. The discovery of gold in the 1850s made Australia's mining industry an important part of its economy. The government kept news quiet about the first discoveries for fear that convicts, soldiers, and servants would leave their duties to hunt for gold. New minerals and elements were discovered in the early 1900s. These included bauxite (the source of aluminum), uranium, oil, and natural gas. Today, 75 percent of items exported to other countries are mining products.

The Fimiston Open Pit, also known as the Super Pit, is the second-largest open pit mine in Australia.

Forestry

The forestry industry in Australia contributes more than $9 billion AUD ($6 billion USD) to the economy. Logs are harvested from native forests and tree plantations. The plantations consist mainly of pine and eucalypts. Logs harvested from Australia's commercial plantations are processed into boards, paper, and paneling. Woodchips are one of Australia's main exports and are sent to China and Japan.

Logs are loaded onto a ship in the port of Hobart, Tasmania, for export.

Pine logs are loaded onto a truck in Tasmania.

Life Today

Happy Life

Australians are known for their "no worries" approach to life. This means to put aside stress and appreciate the good things in life that are right in front of you. Being a good friend and neighbor is also important. Australians pride themselves on **compassion** for those in need. In fact, Australia was named the second most charitable country in the world by the CAF World Giving Index.

Australia ranks consistently high on happiness indexes. This is mainly because the country has low unemployment, strong health care, and a solid education system. Australians also have the highest turnout for voters at 93 percent. This is because voting is **mandatory** and the government works to make it convenient for citizens to vote.

Tourism

Australia is famous around the world for its natural wonders, wide-open spaces, and beaches. Before travel restrictions from the COVID-19 pandemic, more than 9 million people visited Australia each year. The Great Barrier Reef, the Blue Mountains, and Bondi Beach are some of the most visited sites.

Indigenous Australians

Australia's relationship with its Indigenous peoples is complicated. There are often clashes over land and resources. In 1992, the courts recognized the existence of Indigenous land over large parts of rural Australia. However, Indigenous Australians face **prejudice**, and they also struggle with discrimination, violence, racism, poverty, and higher suicide rates. Indigenous groups often battle with the mining industry over resources. Aboriginal and Torres Strait Islander peoples are still not formally recognized in the Australian constitution.

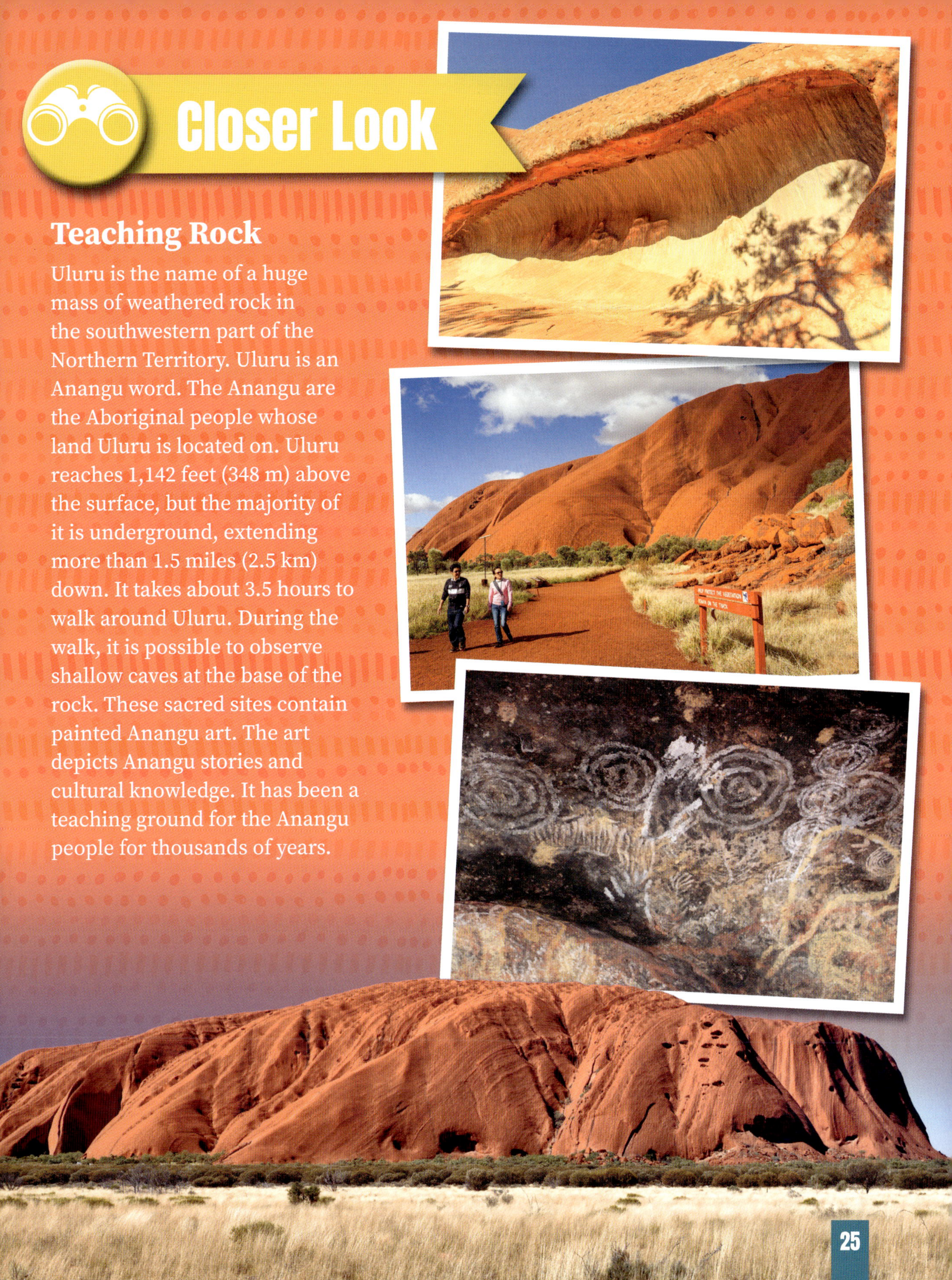

Closer Look

Teaching Rock

Uluru is the name of a huge mass of weathered rock in the southwestern part of the Northern Territory. Uluru is an Anangu word. The Anangu are the Aboriginal people whose land Uluru is located on. Uluru reaches 1,142 feet (348 m) above the surface, but the majority of it is underground, extending more than 1.5 miles (2.5 km) down. It takes about 3.5 hours to walk around Uluru. During the walk, it is possible to observe shallow caves at the base of the rock. These sacred sites contain painted Anangu art. The art depicts Anangu stories and cultural knowledge. It has been a teaching ground for the Anangu people for thousands of years.

There are many places for people to bushwalk in Australia.

With Australia's hot climate and numerous beaches, swimming and surfing are popular pastimes.

Enjoying Nature

The beautiful natural landscape and a passion for nature results in a love of outdoor activities for Australians. With six national parks, 60 marine parks, and 81 Indigenous Protected Areas, there are many places to explore and enjoy the natural beauty of the country.

Bushwalking is a favorite way to discover natural areas. Bushwalking means **self-sufficient** hikes from a day to a week long. There are trails in every national park as well as local bushwalking clubs and tours. One of Australia's toughest bushwalks is the trail to the top of Federation Peak in Tasmania's Eastern Arthur Mountain Range.

People enjoy camping next to Australia's many pink lakes.

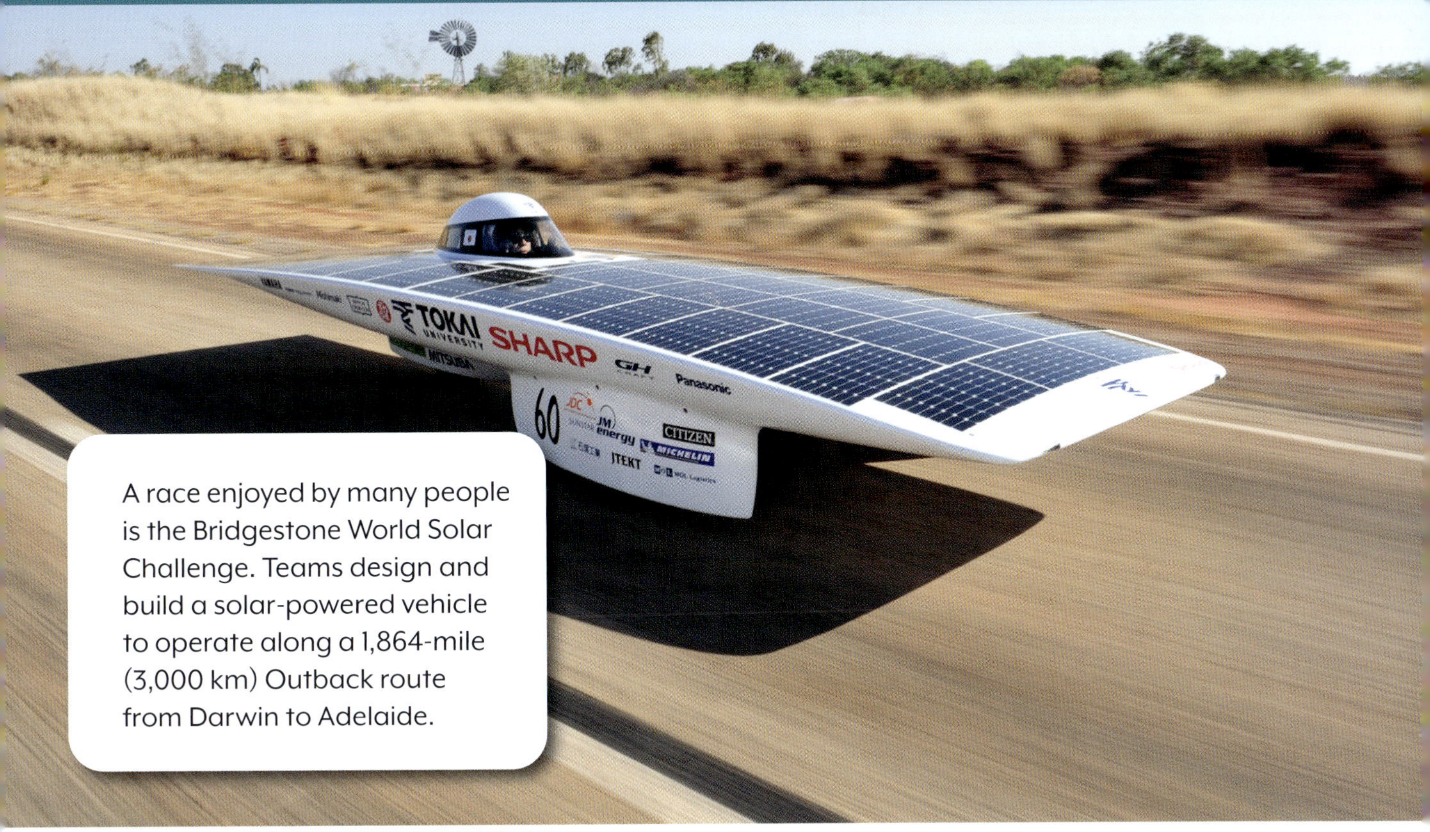

A race enjoyed by many people is the Bridgestone World Solar Challenge. Teams design and build a solar-powered vehicle to operate along a 1,864-mile (3,000 km) Outback route from Darwin to Adelaide.

Sports and Recreation

Camping is not just popular with tourists, but it is also very popular with Australians. With vast unspoiled areas, reliably dry and sunny weather, and native wildlife for company, the number of people camping is increasing each year. Some of the most **secluded** spots in Australia are only accessible to campers and hikers.

The oldest and longest-running motorsport event in Australia is the Alpine Rally, which started in 1921. With Australia's large, open interior plains, this race was first used to test the endurance of cars. It also helped to open up the northeast part of the state of Victoria to tourism. Another motorsport is the Australian Off-Road Championship. It is a long course rally, which means the tracks are at least 9 miles (15 km) long. Australia is a perfect location for this because of the wide, open spaces and different landforms, such as sand dunes, creek crossings, hills, and farmland. Besides the natural landforms, tracks might also have human-made jumps and obstacles.

Opal Mining

The opal mining industry is still growing. People wanting to mine for opals in Australia must pay for a Precious Stone Prospecting Permit, identification plates, and registration of claims. Miners have to take an opal mining course that focuses on first aid, electrical problems, and safety procedures. There are also rules to replant vegetation on the site once the claim permit expires.

Opals are very colorful gemstones.

Mintabie is an opal mining community in South Australia. It is located on traditional Aboriginal lands. The Anangu Pitjantjatjara Yankunytjatjara (APY) people leased the land to the government for 30 years in the 1980s. Valuable white and crystal opals are found in the area. It was one of the richest deposits in Australia. When the lease was up in 2019, miners were **evicted** from the now-abandoned town. Traditional owners of the land plan to fill in all the mining holes and return the land to the way it used to be.

Opal miners drill deep shafts or tunnels underground. The debris is brought up to the surface and put in piles which are then sifted through in search of opals.

Piles of coal wait to be exported at the Port of Hay Point terminal in Queensland.

Digging for Gold

Gold mining is expected to grow in Australia. It is already the second-largest gold producer after China. Eighty percent of gold mining is done on Aboriginal lands. The Aboriginal Land Rights Act of 1976 provides negotiations between Aboriginal groups and resource companies. Traditional owners typically gain protection for sacred and environmental sites as well as employment and training opportunities. Mining companies such as BHP and Rio Tinto are committed to raising the percentage of Aboriginal employees above the current levels of only about 20 percent.

Coal Consumption

While most of the developed world has decreased its coal consumption as it moves to more clean, **renewable** energy, Australia is still mining coal for many developing countries. Australia exported more than $13 billion AUD ($9 billion USD) to China in 2019. In 2020, China put a ban on Australia's coal after tensions arose between the two countries. Since then, Australia has looked to increase its exports to other countries, such as India. Australia is not eager to decrease coal mining or coal consumption because it creates so many jobs and brings in so much money to the economy.

Agriculture

The number of sheep in Australia has fallen from 180 million in the 1970s to about 64 million today. It is the lowest point in 100 years. The cause is said to be from the falling price of wool, droughts, and people's preference for other meats, such as beef. The sheep industry is expecting to **rebound** with growing flocks and higher prices for meat and wool.

The vast grasslands of the tropical and temperate zones are home to the millions of cattle that make up Australia's beef industry. Cattle on the stations live a basically wild life. They freely roam the grass of the cattle stations, which can be thousands of acres large. Anna Creek Station in South Australia is the world's largest cattle station, with over 5,851,000 acres (2,367,816 hectares). Owners of cattle stations are called graziers. A grazier's neighbor can be over a day's drive away. Mail and supplies are delivered by planes. School for kids living on a remote cattle station is called "School of the Air" because lessons used to be delivered by radio. Today, computers and Internet by satellite provide their education.

Stockmen are people who tend to cattle on the stations.

With its mild climate, grain crops can be grown both in the summer and winter in Australia. Winter crops include wheat, barley, and canola. In the summer, farmers grow sorghum, cotton, and sunflowers.

Fishing Industry

Up to 90 percent of Australians eat seafood regularly. The fishing industry in Australia includes commercial fishers, fish farmers, and oyster growers. With fish populations decreasing around the world, Australia is working to keep the fishing industry **sustainable**. It has implemented various ways to help protect other sea creatures, such as sea turtles, from the nets and cables used by fishers. There are also devices used to keep sea birds and fish that are returned to the water safe. To give sport fishers more opportunity, commercial fishing has been prohibited in 30 Recreational Fishing Havens along the NSW coast. Fishing is not allowed at all in the 60 Marine Protected Areas found in the ocean and surrounding coastline of the country. These areas range from small marine reserves to large, multi-use parks, such as the Great Barrier Reef Marine Park.

Tuna is a popular fish caught in Australia.

Grain, such as wheat, is often exported to places such as China and Indonesia.

Scallops are a type of mollusk found in various locations around the coast of Australia.

CHAPTER 4 A Vibrant Country

Because it is in the southern hemisphere, Australia is known in North America as the "Land Down Under." It has many unique features and creatures. Australia is a land with some of the world's biggest, longest, and most dangerous things.

Natural Beauty

Australia has the longest national highway in the world. Highway 1 is 9,010 miles (14,500 km) long and circles the country along the coast. More than a million people travel on some part of it every day. Australia also has more than 10,000 beaches and 8,000 islands for people to enjoy. Kakadu National Park in the Northern Territory is one of the largest national parks in the world. It is also a sacred site for many Aboriginal peoples. It contains many examples of ancient Aboriginal rock art, some of them up to 20,000 years old, making them the longest historical records of any group of people in the world.

Unique Language

Australia has developed its own slant on the English language, with many slang words and phrases unique to the country. Australians often **abbreviate** words, such as "sunnies" for sunglasses, "chooks," for chickens, and "chewie" for chewing gum. Other words, such as "tucker" for food, come from the Irish and British roots of the original convicts. The language is still evolving as young Australians add their own slang terms, such as "bludger," which means someone who is lazy.

Kakadu National Park has more than 5,000 recorded sites featuring ancient Aboriginal art.

The taipan snake is the world's most venomous snake. All three species of this snake can be found in Australia. Its venom is powerful enough to kill a human in a few hours if left untreated.

Some tourists take a detour off Highway 1 to visit the famous Three Sisters rock formation, found in the Blue Mountains National Park just west of Sydney.

Dangerous and Deadly Animals

Some of the world's most dangerous animals live on mainland Australia and the surrounding islands. Deadly snakes, spiders, sharks, and jellyfish are just a few creatures that call Australia home. The saltwater crocodile, which lives in river **deltas** and swamps, is responsible for approximately seven attacks on people per year—some of them fatal. The box jellyfish, found off the northern coast, is said to be the most toxic animal on Earth. Its 15 tentacles that grow to be 10 feet (3 m) long contain 5,000 stinging cells that release venom into its victims. A human or animal can be killed within minutes of being stung. In Australia's southern waters are some small but deadly creatures. The golf ball-sized blue-ringed octopus has enough venom to kill 26 humans in minutes. There is no antivenom for its bite, but a victim can be saved if they receive help with their breathing immediately.

Cultures and Traditions

Australia is a land of different cultures that stem from the traditions and history of the different groups living there. Aboriginal and Torres Strait Islander peoples have lived on the continent for thousands of years. Europeans arrived as crew, passengers, and **captives** on the convict ships. Immigrants from all corners of the world, including Germany, the Netherlands, China, and India, have arrived in recent years to make a new life.

Today, Aboriginal and Torres Strait Islander cultural festivals are celebrated all over the country. Cultural festivals help communities grow and maintain traditions. Corroborees are dance rituals with costumes and music. Music is one way Indigenous peoples share their identity and show their pride in their heritage.

Torres Strait Islanders perform ceremonies in traditional costumes.

During Australia Day celebrations, Aboriginal men perform a traditional dance.

Holidays and Celebrations

Western Australian culture comes from the British and Irish who arrived on its shores starting in 1788. Today, the roots of this culture can be seen in holiday celebrations. Australian Christmas is in the summer and often starts with a surfing Santa and a Christmas lunch that includes **prawns**. Just like in Britain and Canada, the day after Christmas is called Boxing Day. Australians, who call themselves Aussies, spend the day off watching a big cricket match held in Melbourne called the Boxing Day Test.

An important day for all Australians is April 25. This is ANZAC Day. It is a public holiday to remember those who died in military operations. It started in 1916 to honor those serving in World War I (WWI). ANZAC stands for Australia and New Zealand Army Corps. In WWI the two countries joined forces to fight together. Like Memorial Day in the U.S. or Remembrance Day in Canada, it includes ceremonies at war memorials, wreath laying, and a minute of silence.

Christmas crackers are also a fun tradition in Australia.

Veterans wear their war medals when attending ANZAC Day celebrations.

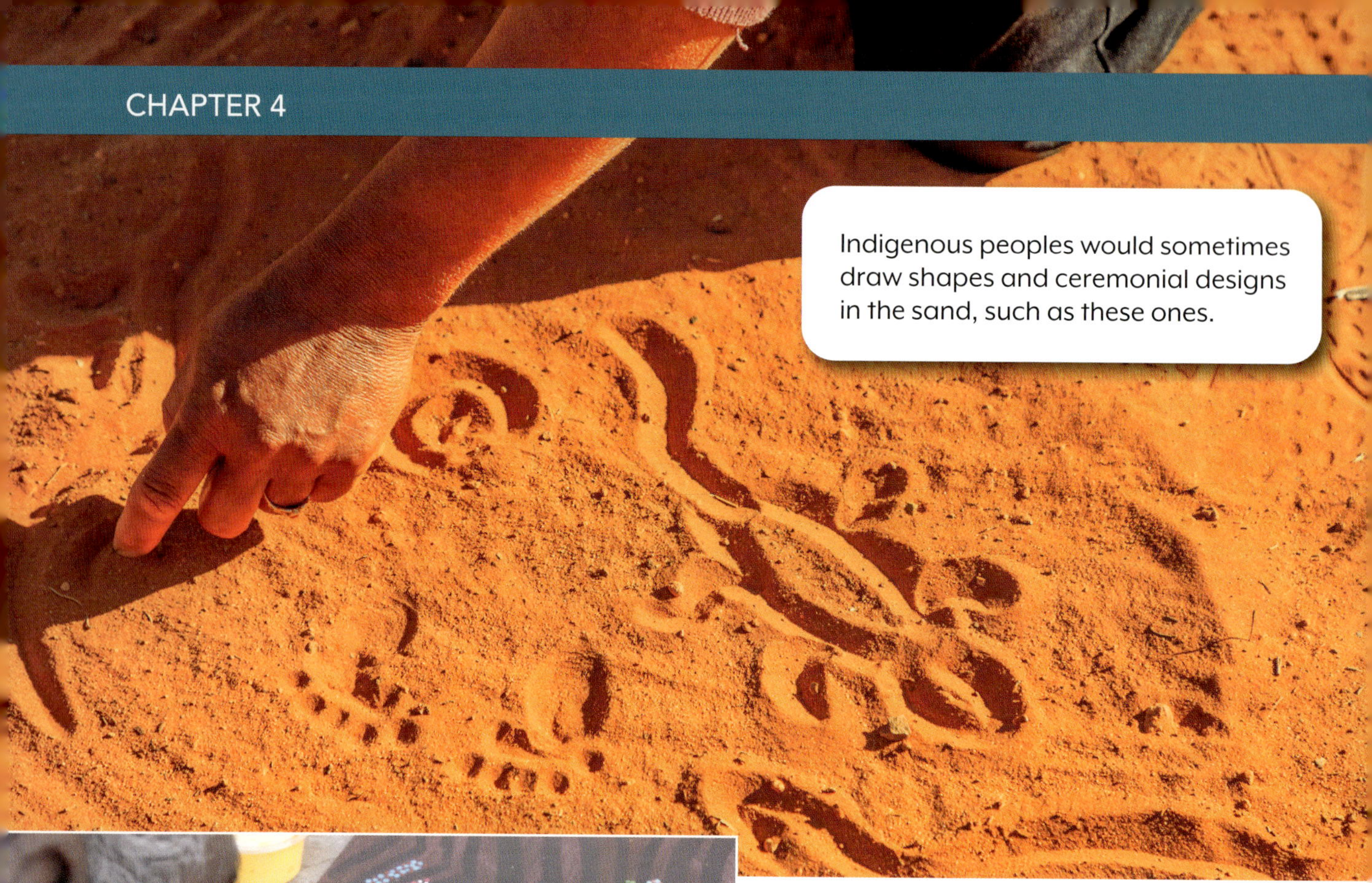

Indigenous peoples would sometimes draw shapes and ceremonial designs in the sand, such as these ones.

Aboriginal artists began using abstract dots so the sacred meanings of the ceremonies and stories told through their paintings would not be understood by others.

Indigenous Art

Art in Australia has been made from prehistoric times to the present day. Modern art is a fusion of the varied cultures and ethnic groups that now live in Australia. The earliest art is found in caves and on the walls of sacred Indigenous sites.

Australian Indigenous peoples had no written language. To pass on ancient stories and ideas they used symbols and pictures. Indigenous peoples mined for ochre, a red rock that is crushed and mixed with oil to make paint. It was used on rocks and bark and as body paint. Body and face paint were used as a way for some Indigenous peoples to show social status, **ancestry**, geography, and family groups. It was often done around the time of marriage ceremonies. The oldest wall painting is an ochre picture of a kangaroo in the Kimberley region.

The Sydney Opera House is one of the most recognizable buildings in the world. It is famous for its white sail-like roofline. It is a location for performing arts such as symphony, theater, and dance.

A musician performs with a traditional didgeridoo.

Music and Dance

Australia has developed its own music and dance styles. Indigenous instruments are unique to the country. The didgeridoo is a long wooden tube that is blown into like a flute. The bull-roarer is a heavy piece of wood at the end of a long rope that is swung to make noise. Clapsticks are like drumsticks, and make a sound when hit together. Australian folk music is a combination of different immigrant cultures such as British, Celtic, German, and Scandinavian.

Bush dance is a dance style from Australia. It is based on traditional folk dances from Britain, Ireland, and central Europe. The music is often provided by a bush band. Some of the instruments of a typical bush band are the fiddle, accordion, guitar, banjo, and tin whistle.

Reclaiming Heritage

Aboriginal peoples view the world through their Dreamtime stories. These tales, passed down through generations, tell of the importance of sharing and caring for people. They also stress the importance of nurturing the land.

Indigenous peoples lost much of their culture with the arrival of the convict ships and other immigrants. Their land was taken and their hunter-gatherer lifestyle was restricted. Moving to more urban areas meant a loss of skills, culture, lifestyle, and identity for Indigenous peoples. Today, many of them are moving back to Indigenous communities in remote areas. This is known as "the outstation movement." It is an attempt to reoccupy traditional clan lands, and relearn skills and traditions.

Basket weaving using local materials is one tradition of Indigenous Australians.

Honey ants have been a source of sugar for many Aboriginal peoples in the Northern Territory and Western Australia. Holes are dug into the ground to gather the ants.

People from India are one of the fastest-growing immigrant groups in Australia. Many Indian cultural events are celebrated in Australian cities, such as the Festival of Colors, called Holi, in Melbourne.

Australian Ancestors

Australians have mixed feelings about their convict heritage. About 20 percent of mainland Australians and 74 percent of people living in Tasmania are descended from the original convicts. At first, having convict ancestry was a secret to be kept quiet at all costs. No one wanted to be thought of as a criminal. Records with convict names were guarded. Now it is almost a matter of pride to have a connection to them. Many have negative attitudes toward the British ruling class that punished the poor and needy for **petty** crimes. Many convicts turned their lives around and helped found a **prosperous democracy**.

CHAPTER 5 Looking to the Future

The future holds challenges for Australia. New technology, scientific discoveries, and a changing world will impact jobs, health, and industry. The Australia 2050 project is a plan to help Australia chart its path into the future. It brings scientists and experts together to answer questions about society, the environment, and being sustainable.

Indigenous Protection Areas are Indigenous owned or managed land. Managers work closely with Parks Australia. IPAs are part of the National Reserve System's network to protect the nation's **biodiversity**. At present there are 81 IPAs, but more are planned.

Protecting the Reef

The Great Barrier Reef is under enormous pressure. With more tourists and visitors each year, there is more pollution and damage to the reef. Warming oceans from climate change are causing larger and more frequent bleaching events. Bleaching happens when the coral **expels** the microscopic organisms that live in its walls. This makes the coral look white, or "bleached." These organisms help provide food for the coral. If the bleaching event lasts too long, the coral can starve to death.

Runoff from the coast also affects the reef. Runoff is the extra water flowing down rivers and streams into the ocean after heavy rains. It can contain high levels of chemicals and fertilizers from farmland and gardens. These extra **nutrients** can cause the crown-of-thorns starfish population to increase quickly. These starfish are the second biggest cause of damage to the Great Barrier Reef after bleaching. To help control them, divers remove a large number of starfish from the reef.

Rangers in the Dhimurru Indigenous Protected Area in the Northern Territory teach visitors traditional fire-making skills.

Closer Look

Government Help

The Reef Trust is an Australian government investment program that helps support the Reef 2050 Long-Term Sustainability Plan. The plan was established to help protect the reef until the year 2050. Some of the Reef Trust projects focus on improving water quality around the reef and protecting threatened species that migrate to and from the reef, such as dugongs and sea turtles. Other projects are working to reduce land runoff, control the crown-of-thorns starfish population, and keep the ecosystems on the coast healthy. The Australian government has committed $1.3 billion AUD ($900 million USD) to the Reef Trust program.

Divers must be careful not to touch the crown-of-thorns starfish when removing it. The thorns can cause severe pain, stinging, and swelling for hours or even days.

Dugongs can be found at the reef. They have a fluke-like tail like a dolphin, unlike their cousin the manatee that has a rounded, paddle-shaped tail.

Future of Farming

Farming and livestock are being affected by climate change. There are increased and longer-lasting droughts each year in Australia. Some sheep and cattle farmers do not have enough grassland to support their flocks and herds. Some farmers are turning to growing crops instead. Research farms are testing different kinds of wheat, fava beans, and chickpeas to select types that can handle drier conditions. Some farmers are using digital maps to pick areas of their farms that have better soil and water conditions to grow crops.

University of Adelaide researchers are working on a new way of removing fleece from sheep without shearing. Shearing can be expensive, and is sometimes uncomfortable for the sheep if they are accidentally cut. There is also often a shortage of experienced shearers. Chemical defleecing means treating the wool so fibers are weakened just above the skin. Simple machines can then remove the fleece by applying energy at weak points and removing the fleece with no risk of cuts to the skin.

Modern-Day Mining

Mining in Australia is also changing. Even though coal is continuing to be mined, mining for metals and minerals needed for green energy is increasing. Lithium is a mineral that is used in batteries. Lithium batteries contain fewer **toxic** metals and are better for the environment. Many mines are also making the mining process greener with better **e-waste** recycling and lower carbon emissions from mining vehicles.

The Australian minerals industry is also participating in the Towards Sustainable Mining program. TSM was developed in Canada and is a way of judging how well a mine is improving in terms of pollution, community, safety, and protecting the environment. The guidelines score the mines on their relationships with Indigenous communities, clean water projects, conserving the land, and meeting climate change targets.

Cows gather in a dried-up riverbed during a period of drought in Australia.

A processing plant at a lithium mine in Western Australia uses a mechanical process to refine spodumene ore to produce the lithium needed for batteries.

Children gather at a climate change protest at their school in Melbourne.

Changes and Challenges

Australia is also facing a growing gap of services, opportunities, health, and welfare between those living in cities and those in rural areas. Children living in remote areas do not participate in as many clubs and sports. Children in urban areas often have better education, leading to more job opportunities when they are older.

Closing the Gap is a program funded by the Australian government that started in 2007. Its goal is to work toward equality for Aboriginal and Torres Strait Islander peoples in health care, education, and jobs. Early childhood education is increasing to give children in rural areas a strong beginning. Other goals are increasing the number of Indigenous students finishing high school and helping them access college or university.

Asian Immigrants

More people are migrating to Australia. Immigrants from Asian countries now make up a larger portion than European-born immigrants. This will change the religious landscape, festivals, languages, and culture of the country. Mandarin Chinese is now the second most-common spoken language in Australia after English.

Areas that show a strong Chinese cultural identity are called Chinatowns. They can be found in most Australian states and territories.

Promoting Tourism

Australia is working to boost tourism following the COVID-19 pandemic. The Aussie Specialist Program (ASP) is a course for travel agents in other countries to learn more about Australia. They are trained online to be better able to sell Australian vacations and tours. The tourism industry is also encouraging locals to travel and discover their country.

Indigenous tourism is also growing. Indigenous guides show visitors around traditional lands and share art, music, and food. Indigenous tourism in Queensland is becoming so popular that the tourism board is planning on creating a new Queensland Indigenous tourism council. The chance to experience a "new" old culture is drawing even more tourists to the "Land Down Under."

An Indigenous man gives tourists information about bush plants used in traditional ceremonies.

A tourist in Queensland gets a lesson on boomerang throwing.

abbreviate To shorten

ancestry Your family tree

arid Having very little rain or water

biodiversity The different kinds of life in an environment

captives People held against their will

cays Low islands of coral reefs, rock, or sand

compassion Concern for others

compatible Able to be used together

controversial A subject or opinion that people disagree about

delta A triangle-shaped sandy area at the mouth of a river

democracy A system of government where all the eligible people vote for who represents them

densely Close together

drainage basin Area where rainwater collects and flows down to a body of water

emitted Given off

evicted Forced to leave an area

e-waste Broken or unwanted electronic products

expels Pushes something out

exported Sold to another country

flammable Easily catches fire

fleece The woolly covering of a sheep

foraged Went into nature to look for food

illiterate Unable to read or write

Indigenous peoples The original inhabitants of a place

mandatory Required by a rule or law

monsoon A shift in winds that often causes a very rainy season or a very dry one

nutrients The elements needed to grow and stay healthy

penal colony A settlement where prisoners are sent to live

petty Not serious

prawns Small sea animals similar to shrimp

prejudice Dislike for people without good reason

prosperous Wealthy and successful

rebound To return from a bad situation

renewable A source that is not used up

rock shield Large area of very old rock under the soil

secluded Sheltered and private

self-sufficient Having all the things you need with you

semi-arid desert Dry area that gets less than 20 inches (50 cm) of rain each year

silica Element found in the ground made of silicon and oxygen

southern hemisphere The part of Earth that is south of the equator

sustainable Able to last for a long time

temperate Having temperatures that are not too hot and not too cold

toxic Poisonous

treaty A formal, written agreement between two groups

tropical Having warm temperatures year round

UNESCO World Heritage site A protected landmark or area singled out by the United Nations Educational, Scientific, and Cultural Organization as being globally significant

vegetation Plant life

Books

Colson, Mary. *Indigenous Australian Cultures.* Heinemann, 2012.

Medina, Nico. *Where is the Great Barrier Reef?* Penguin, 2016.

Morganelli, Adrianna. *Pathways Through Australia.* Crabtree Publishing, 2020.

Websites

Explore Australia with National Geographic Kids:
https://kids.nationalgeographic.com/geography/countries/article/australia

Take a virtual tour of the Great Barrier Reef with David Attenborough:
https://attenboroughsreef.com/

Learn more about Indigenous Australians with Kiddle:
https://kids.kiddle.co/Indigenous_Australians

Check out the patterns and symbols used in Aboriginal art:
https://art-educ4kids.weebly.com/aboriginal-art-and-patterning.html

Index

About the Author

Natalie Hyde has written over 100 fiction and non-fiction books for young readers. Exploring new cultures, traditions, and of course, food, is something she loves to do on her travels.